A.K.A. Peter Coco

At the Hop

Recent Poems
2012–2015

Peter Cocuzza

Ohayo Press
Woodstock, New York

Printed in the United States of America

Distribution by Epigraph Publishing Service

Library of Congress Control Number: 2016900862

ISBN: 978-1-944037-18-5

Book design by Colin Rolfe

.

Ohayo Press
Woodstock, N.Y.

Table of Contents

At The Hop

----

the Jitterbug gait
of consciousness
is a Twist twirling
Boogaloo
that does
The Bump…
occasionally knudging
The Lovers
on their
Slow Grind
across the universe

I Saw You

I Know You Were There
I Saw You

Your Mother
Got Nasty With The Cops
Like She Always Did
And You Went Back
To The Basement
After The Fracas
And Continued Screwing
Beverly Davis –
The Finest Black Girl
In Grammar School –
Her Long Legs
Wrapped Around
Your Neck –
I Saw That Too
From The Side
Of The Doorway –
Wow! That Was
Something For A Kid
Like Me – Still Looking
For A Kiss!

The Day After
Me And Your Sister
Won 2nd Place
In The Twist Contest,
You Stepped In DogShit
With Your New Wingtips…
I Saw It And Called
You "Shitshoe" Loudly
In Our 7th Grade Class
You Had Just Been
Transferred To From
Reform School

You Banged Me
In The Face For That

And I Understood
That Our Best Friendship
Was Over

…And Now For
The Hard Part…
I Was There
On The Street
When Your Crippled
Father Beat You
So Bad With His Cane
Out Onto The Stoop
Of Your Building
And You Ran Up
The Fire Escape
5 Stories
To The Roof
And Stayed There
At The Edge, Shivering
In Your Pajamas,
In A Big Blizzard.
Your Mother
Called The Cops
And They Got You Down
And Warned Your Father.

When I Saw That,
I Knew That You
Were Worse-Off
Than Me And
Always Would Be

****

Over The Next
Dozen Or So Years
I Wrote 3 Poems
Wondering About
You In Jail
And Whether You
Were Out Yet:

One On A Canal
Barge In Amsterdam,
One From An Oasis
In The Sinai,
One From A Coutyard
In The City Of Thanjavur –
I Asked Myself
About The Luck
Of Freedom –
Why Me And Not You?
Afterall, You Were The
Brave One.

When I Returned
Home, You Were On The
Front Page
Of The News
Along With Your
Brother And Sister –
Busted Kidnapping
The Richest Man
In America.

I Saw That
I Saw You

Now Everyone Did,
Even Me

Henri's Table

Bad Buddha Sez
'Anything That Happens
Happens Once And Forever
And Across The Universe
Simultaneous-Like'
        so…
                There's A Window
                In The Door

                Tiptoed Paper Cuts
                Mark The Wind
                On Sly

                Black Hole Stashes
                Cote D'Azur Dazzle

                Groomed Beards
                Escher Jungle Canopy

                Straw Hat Tips
                On Ice

                Noh Rambles
                The Midi

Wiseguy Einstein's
Just Figured Out
That Nothing Can
Exist Without
The Perception
Of The Perciever
        i.e….
                Turn Your Back On The Wall – It's Gone!
ergo…
        Monsieur Matisse,
        You Have Express
        Permission To Use
        My Kitchen
        Whenever I Am
        Not Around

The Bear Never Shows 'Til Dawn

I was carrying my brother's child
that he had given me on the way
down the stairs of a nightclub...
I held the child up
in the palm of my buff-polished
cowhide glove – like it was on a tray –
the slightest of things – it was about
¾" tall, skinny as a newborn salamander
and seemed to have two arms like dolphin fins
protruding from assymetric parts of it's torso...
I could see it clearly smiling with guppy eyes
from it's wormlike head...it was so light
I could not feel it in my hand and for an instant
I worried if it was safe with me like that...
and as we approached a porch, a little breeze
passed through and I wondered if the child
had gotten blown out of my hand...and when
I looked, it was gone...
I checked all around me and quickly dropped
to the ground and searched in spirals...I saw an
eensie bird about the child's size and thought that
it might be the child in another way and maybe I
could bring it back instead, but in a second I knew
that would not work...
I went back into the night club and began tracing
my steps...a beaver laid flat and made me jump
over him as he handed me a small, plastic flashlight...
I slid, combing the dirty floors, down the old steps, then
dropped the flashlight into a murky puddle beneath
a half-open grating just short of the sidewalk...
I reached down for it and pulled up a blue mouse
with it that plopped back down and splashed my face...
on all fours, I scoured the sidewalk – side to side –
end to end – a porcupine reared up in front of me
near the porch that was fading – I guessed that my
entourage had gone into the house – a baby turtle tugged my
left sleeve like he knew something – my stingy-brim hat
fell off, hooking onto my nose...I tried to see it...
right then, a very bright light drew me awake.

The Bear Never Shows 'Til Dawn

I Do Not Bid Them Understand

Everybit
here before
in place
summoned
somewhere else
we do not know
by hands
that never touch
voice never
spoke.
down river
never flow
boat filled
in element departed
from dream
of soul
forgotten
until I see your Face

Empty Hallway

----

ceiling pock
old bed
pajama race
tree blink
stocking dig
paper rip
box pop
plastic rattle
metal grind
feet pound
floor creak

shoe shine
cufflink
passed suit
new tie
ancient pin
Brylcreem
brim hat

stone church
hard kneel
mass song

picture near stoop

granma
granpa
salutation
goomba
gooma
papa
mama
dialect explosion
sit

other room
card table
child princess
child jerk
dressed to kill

skadole soup
antipasto
raviola
meatball
braciol
sausage sweet
sausage hot

green salad
whole bird
5 vegetable

fruit crunch
nut crack
fennook

t.v. men
crazy kids
women dishes dish

coffee
expresso
ricotta pie
cake
pumpkin pie
biscotti
honey twist
butter cookie
sugar cookie
struvela
macaroon

men sleep t.v.
women dishes dish
kids hide

Sinatra
King Cole
menthe
cacao
anisette

expresso
anisette cookie

good night paisan

pajama
Scrooge
Scrooge
late Scrooge
tree off
good night

Gone
Gone
all Gone
along with
the agita

Kid Galahad

----

breadwinner gone
by wheelbarreled bricks
fallen on face of tall father
just shy of The Crash
       left as always been
       to son eldest - this time You –
       to make up the difference…

recent of patriation must eat…
and no way back to Sicily.

    8 rounds 50 times
    3 rounds 200 times
        if you won
        you got a gold watch
        you pawned to feed them…
if you lost
you got nothing…
      your only luck:
      a southpaw.

     'guess that is what "Hall Of Fame"
     is all about.

Kind Quiet Boxer
there are no more of you
in this wayward linked globe.

    "left right Left! jab jab jab
    right cross! bend your knees
    – left hook!
  cover your face! jab jab jab
  right! jab jab
      Keep Your Jab Up!
      Keep Your Jab Up Son!!

His gentle laugh at my awkward attempts
keeps me trying…

Birthday 8
got real trunks
with guinea t
to match
      real gloves
      1st sneaks…
                he sat on stool facing me
                paddle mit on each hand
                held palm to me, fielding
                each hit he called,
            hashing out the rules of The Game
step by punch
under the stairwell
of the common hallway
                out of way
            of evil eye spooked
wife/mother
      who cut up and threw out the uniform
     forbidding practice in rage fit
   after 4 sessions only
             denying me something
             more than an abstract of
             this man
             who tried to teach me
             the only thing
             that he knew
who would never have anything else
to tell me or show me
             years turn decades
             turn long lives
                strangers
…as if that were normal.

now, as I see him in last room to witnees
his last event – featured for no crowd –
in last hospital bed
            mis-matched, battling

way up-weight contender,
Pugilistic Dementia –

>   jaw open-close cranking
>   dry tounge gibbered
>   mumble-stutter
>   non-stop neck
>   swiveled head roll
>   light eye palor
>   strapped down
>   contort jump snap
>   jamming back
>   to sequence same

over and over
and over again
relentless hour to hour...

no one could have cherished his short, sly laugh like I did,
a tear of joy welled now, as my final turn look
at his incomprehensible incomprehensibly wailed existence

I say what I know I mean:

"Keep Your Jab Up Dad"

and for the very splitest of seconds
I hear from deeper than the strung-out
babble of dying, - clear as a bell -
that same sly laugh
that I now inherit and revel;
closet full of Birthday trunks lined-up.

I Knew You When

I knew You When
Everyday Abondanza
Every day had Human Beings
included – calm to storm –
always huddled –

I knew you when Fun
was an empty
refrigerator box,
a bottle cap
or snow higher
than a street sign

I knew you
when a good
'45 was a miracle
and Rock & Roll
was "…anything
with a drumbeat",
church was expected
school hurt so bad
and cops knew you
well enough to
catch you running –
the sky was only escape,
cars were not the main vehicle,
people worked 'til they got home…
and *no one* was on the street…

I knew you when you
were old and young
at the same time
like an egg,
restless and dead,
ordinary and alone,
invested and abandoned

I knew you when you were
full, then emptied,
with nothing but Racism
to blame…

Old Newark, I knew you when
you broke
my heart
burning
under
my
wings

Reesey's Quarter

"Tho Me Pinny!
I Tho You Cwata!"

Reesey looks like he
slept on his head
scratches his bare
stomach stuck-out
4 year old packed
in brick house apartment
next to Saint Antoninus church
with 5 other families
fresh up from the Black South
(so the Goomas say),
barging into another breed
of immigrant
on 8th Street
near South Orange Avenue
in old and dying anyway
Newark 1958.

"Tho Me Pinny…
I Tho You Cwata!"

What?

I have a penny.
I bottle beonguline bleach
into glass gallons
from a spigot
in an open cement tank
down Frank Mazulli's cellar
across the street
for 10 cents a day.

Where is Reesey gonna
get a quarter anyway
if he is asking me for
a penny everday?

"**Tho** Me Pinny!...
I Tho You *Cwata*!!"

I imagine Little Reesey
snugging himself
into a corner of a room
with a lot of people
and noise,
his skinny, wild-haired
mother calling him loud
for dinner –
he stays still
as long as he can –
Hungry -
already lit out
for Promised Land.

maybe that quarter
is something
I will never spend

Provincetown
(to Pete)

I went back and saw the place
you cursed me with goodbye
the night before The Kent State
Massacre...as if you had had a
premonition that the 'Hippie
Movement' had become too
dangerous...and that it scared
you enough to admit to yourself
that I would be alone with my
head from here on

I went back to the room
the world tilted with
it's own trouble -
the one where your face
went from flesh to stone
and in one glance,
my heart broke shunned -
leperized from our youth together -
taken from sense and feeling -
forced to surrender our laughs,
release the safety of our bond
and suffer the things
that only we two know

I went back to the fireplace
we huddled, guests of
our saviors, at the end
of this end road rambled
through blind fog
as fast as Angels would fly -
disallusion to dissonance -
Peace Love and Everybody's business
to nobody's –
South Orange Avenue
to Commercial Street solid -
just like always –

Proud from alley/rooftop/corner/
schoolyard/hustle/fence/
'Nicky Newark'/wiseguy rule/
Village Beat Cool/
Acid/Barefoot/Brave
Longhaul Groovin'
Best Friend Legend
'Pete & RePete'
Coast To Coast
Invincible

I went back to this
wilded place -
traced of dream
and faith -
curled with time
and your death
to redeem a moment -
our last -
crashing a fate frozen
with birth,
the day before yesterday -
brought with many many
more miles -
stopped at longshore dock
for you -
gone at horizon walk
for me
Blood Brothers lit out
from Pilgrim's first land
ever

Jimmy Carter Wore Shades

Jimmy Carter wore shades
To the 'I Have A Dream'
50th Anniversary podium

he looked like a spy

or a stern news anchor

or a famous author
granted political asylum

or a hitman

or a widower

and because he
did not stop there
to beat his chest,
plate-up platitude,
mimic outrage
or claim his place

nor pat anyone on the back
for 'doing the right thing'
or 'giving it their all'
or getting locked-up
or winning an election,

you had to take notice
when he seemed to interrupt with
a specific list
of current high crimes
and atrocities
slung and dropped
on people of color
everyday
today
tomorrow
as he asked no question

but stated loud
again and again:
"We all know what
Dr. King would
have done
about this"
           detailing
each shame
belting them out
broadside a crowd
weighted in acquiescence
waiting for Obama –

across The Mall
a high granite statue
of Long Gone Negro Martin
beamed startling like a lighthouse
along the feathered shoreline
of two travelled Georgia Souls

Belated Greetings From Asbury Park
(After Superstorm Sandy—Late Summer, 2013)
----

petit nappy 5 year old
mulatto girl sprints chasing to play with skinny 6 year old white boy
and skinny 6 year old black boy
as the two tumble on eachother soaring up and down
the mounded beach like one sideways creature
- their interlocked hands forming a wiggling folding/unfolding arch
that she runs through whenever she catches up - arms shooting the sky blue

the 5 year old bikini'd blonde pixie screams for effect
scampering two feet into the oncoming surf -
and each time it pulls out she dashes back in glee to kiss her baby brother
looking on from their mother's lap in a low beachchair just behind
- over and over and over and over and over -
as if the tide were just an excuse to teach him The Joy Of Love

with a large shovel, slow and deliberate,
one of the grandfathers digs a grave for the eldest son,
then buries him to the neck for 15 minutes
until the young man decides to push free
to join the grandfather who has just lickedy-split
finished a medieval tower of sand
then all the children of two families gather there
and build a city of moated staircased castles
all around the tower, with hand, spade and bucket
- drawing the marvel of anyone near or passing

- a woman who looks Iranian
in big dark shades pulled back dark hair
and skirted bright bathing suit weaves at water's edge through kids
of three nationalities and four colors
feeding them slices of what looks like turkey cold cut
she rolls up and aims into their proned chick/guppie-like mouths,
as they take a break in the action, jogging in place

single seat flying machines buzz back and forth over the near shore
- a little further out - three seat parachutes yanked by speedboats rise and dip
with almost heard yelps of the strapped in riders
- white sails beyond are still with distance - horizon lined up circling

stocky scrawny fatty people of every turn
do not shame themselves with shame
but let the sun be their mirror - handsome happy -

life-guards out of season, small shells skid descent to chest
in rolling current crisp...jump high and dive like a dolphin!...
ride the crest like a champ!...float as if weightless
- half an eye on a recovering sea trying to remember it's place

JFK & Me

Kal Katz entered
the mensroom
at lunchtime
while I was in
the stall successfully
getting myself back
into my high suit pants
after peeing…
He said to an acquaintance
who was drying his hands,
"Strong, No?", I guessed
referring to the smell of
my urine after a long night
closing…maybe they were
talking about something else –
either way, I was hoping that
they did not recognize my shoes.
Kal was always jovial and most
days in his midget baseball cap –
the kind very rich people wear
sailing.
I always looked at him as old
because he was gray and exuded
eruditeness and authority – but
he wasn't much older than me –
just in a completely different
position – he lunched
with Jackie Kennedy
from time to time.
I gave them Table 43,
from where they could see
and not be seen…
looking back, I think
they were an item

Jackie Kennedy
once speeded her
step across the Parking Lot
at Martha's Vineyard Airport
until she was right in my face
all lit up

at just the moment
I had to turn away to get back
in my car.

My Floor Manager
told me that she saw
Jackie Kennedy
project a 5 inch stream
of clear snot from her nose,
then snort it right back up
without batting an eyelash,
before anyone else could
notice, on her way out
of a Garden Room
publishing luncheon.

I once served John Jr.
a Ginger Ale at Caroline's
30th Birthday Party...
he looked at me from
across the bar
with all the irony
I could imagine packed into
his Adonis frame – seeming
at home with the Tragedy
I hoped I was happy
to see him enough not to hint,
as he turned, adoring his sister –
all dressed-up and dancing with
her friends.

I walked out
on bail from
a Federal Courtroom
in Manhattan
with my bloody overcoat
over a hospital gown - head
bandaged and limping –
looked up and the first
thing I saw was John Jr.'s
eyes gazing at me - him dapper
heading into the commissary.
He looked like he recognized me.

I saw my Sicilian born and raised
father, for the first and only time,
up late at night listening to
a bedside radio. He stayed up
until he heard the 1960
Democratic National Convention
nominate JFK.

I got a penny in my change
with JFK's profile pressed
into it between Abraham Lincoln's
neck and the mint date. I saved it
until it was somehow lost in
a renovation 40 years later. I found
out recently, calling an NPR coin
expert that they were common
and maybe worth $2.

My first essay was "John F. Kennedy –
Humanitarian or Politcian ?", in which
I documented him swerving his car
dangerously to avoid hitting a squirrel
on Nantucket.

Alan Young, glazed eyed jumping,
came bounding down the steps
into sophomore High School cafeteria,
spitting on my sleeve as his head
snapped my way with a nervous
wide smiled giggle, yelping:
"Kennedy Got Killed!!!
Kennedy Got Shot!!!
They Shot Him In Texas
With Machine Guns!!!
Johnson Is Dead Too!!!"
Thus, the first iteration
of America's broken heart
pavane – still somber.

Shizuko Yamamoto used
JFK's picture as an example
of Sampaku Eyes

at the first East-West Center
we built near Time Square.

The last time I saw John Jr.
was just before lunch time.
He was walking fast down
W.55th…I guessed on his way
to 'Cote Basque'. I stepped
out to the sidewalk from my
Maitre'd podium and said,
"Come Back".
He turned, recognizing me
and said, " I will, I will".

coatcheck

I used to wish
upon a hammock star
for your possession

now dandruff
almost sparkles
on my black T-Shirt -
    ...looks pretty similar
    to that sky -
and makes me wonder
if I was just wondering
what it would be like
to Have something
free of rebuke
to play with –
to transfer your knock-out smile
and teenage curiosity
    to compulsion
    to easy access
met by my ability to fool you
into thinking that I loved you...

if
wicked
dandruff can teach
bad
Breath can forgive

Untitled

Absorbing The River
I Noticed You Were Gone
I Think That's What Gave
Me A Headache,
I Never Get Headaches…
That Was Two Days Ago –
I Still Have A Headache

Maybe If I Sleep In
I Will Be Able To
Eat Again…
Nothing Tastes…
I Am Bloated…
I Have No Memory –
Only You At Every Turn
As If I Had Just Missed You
Just Missing You

on the way back from Timbuktu

on the way back from Timbuktu
I saw you
passing the other way
on a platform
across two tracks
on a different line
you looked mean
and desperate

I caught your eye
just as your train
pulled in
then out
as if we weren't
man and wife

Cloud Cover

----

some people say
that the stars
are the souls
of the departed.

if they are even
fractally correct,
I am quite
grateful
for cloud cover

Hee-Haw

I saw a naked man
on Madison Avenue today

somehow he had
tied his dick
in a knot around one foot
and hopped with the other

for balance he waved
both arms slow
like an Egret taking off
while stretch scooping
his tounge in time

when he got a 'Don't Walk'
signal, he laid on the ground
waiting for someone to
help him up
or just rolled
across the street
when the light turned
and waited for someone
to give him a hand up there

in steady business rush
sharp of gait
nose prone
dick like I said
knotted to one foot
eyes straight ahead
no blinking
he reached his lunch
sidewalk table
at chic bistro,
untied his dick
and sat down
with his Ass
already there
raving Pate' Mousse

Wall Of Sound
(Phil Spector)
----

tickled pink
room dwelled
groovists
travelling hi
like mighty
lanes forcast
at speeds fortold
proclaim-divine
reverb downbeat
life insurance
issued on summer
hot night
…vibes toll roll
light horn
tall fall
smash drum
hush pop
guitar set
rhythmn cling
as voice
from softer nowhere
cool cranks trance home
sharpharp

ketel one

Sounders passed by
to see what it would be
like to be you...or me

they reported back
to the Maji
    that "...yes, it could be done
        but it wouldn't be
        very much fun..."

"since all we really
need is The Juice,
      why not just
      take it all
    and dispense
with excuse?"

"if embodiment
were successful
there is no safety
    from the whole
    human messfull"-

"with business to
keep up with
    just to keep
    up the front,
pain and pleasure
would be part
of the stunt" -

    "an act so clear
    that it must convince
would bring temptation
to the job as well as wince"

"who knows what these
dramas spiraled
    in eternity
    would cost?

and behind the stage curtain
The Juice could be lost"

"so why take the chance?
let's lift it all now
and scroll back to
stringysphere growtons
and graow"

        The Magi
        were convinced
        of the verity
        of their pleas
but knew that
The Juice itself
could not survive
the Curse of Ease,

for what necessity's fear
would claim
            is slow poison
            by another name.

                ****

they are at the bar amoung us now –
                a flight
                a tumbler
                a bottle
                a shot –
        with The Magi's
        blessing
        for saving
        their lot.

The Old Neighborhood

Madison Square Gyps You Blind
With Flatiron Gotham Promise

only to be run down
on 23rd street ducking
schlock-shop cacophony
all the way to
Original Gramercy Park,
locked in reverie tease -
listless and sneakable
iron-speared pristine ballsack
of once was City

square, circled empty
Braque-clipped images
bobbing between fence bars
framed and varieagated each step
-up and down around park like
carousel horses, pumping breath,
cling and rupture of Long Shot
And Gone –
sharing Banished,
winnowing Forgotten…

cops in their car
slow patrol 21st St.,
the blue, darkened
men inside pretend
they are following me.

A giant mastiff hound gallops by
without a master

February bare,
The Park whistles
Danger in Refuge -
nervous townhouses
classically huddled
around Chill

Big Al Fresco

He eats his kischkes
               out for lunch
               on sidestreet tables
               turned on law-abiding
               citizen's pocket pools
               of sweat shop change,
games the system
 he wrist watches
  like nothing is happening
   to anyone out in The Square
    rounded-up scared,
               with only squeezed
               eyes watching straight
               for any opportunity
               to pay down their note

Big Al flicks ring pinky
sipping his expresso
over Daily News.

the general died at daunt

Dingus Douherty
      ducked
over the fence
    he was leaning
        away
watching his eyes
    close
      crawling under pipe
he laid at length
    turning rattling
      neighbor's
  goose
    cooking
smelling
  himself
    tiptoeing backwards
        people
everyday winnowing
    picnic partners shouting
tempted drooling
    fishermen descending
      scales
belted out by fat ladies
    pasted
      framed
he sits without
   doubt
    front row
      ticketed
        in handicapped
          space
          your
          steps
          with
          feet

Squash Court

King Pumpkin
was wondering
how long it would take
for Queen Butternut
to knock something over
with her fat ass,
while Princess Pattypan
assured Prince Deilicato
that his secret
was safe with her
as the Acorn Wizard
pondered his next move –
Heirlooms wrinkled at
Gagootz and Calabash
protruding –
then Captain Zucchini
got yellow
when Sweet Lord Spaghetti
rolled in from the heat, ripe -
split himself open
and layed himself down
like it was Pasta Night
All You Can Eat

ol flatop

                              He
Stygmied & landlocked
white shirt
white bell pantsf
white pizza
boots lavender purple suede
drape thick hair brown

whole9yardbulge
knudged toward end
of girder plank
                          gives it a whirl

    cleans house
    no prisoners
    before speaks

                    trusted like a bone
                    because alone
                    and must know something
        or
      anything
    Forever.

we listen hard and secret
  like ghosts at Tea.

Briefly

Buddha seeks cover
wishful hearing
himself quake
without a cause

He must eat
so he limits
the menu to
what he loves
before heading out
at unmatchable clip
for the laundry
where everything fits
excluding underwear

dreidel

I saw 16 prophets
milling about in a circular
atrium hovering above,
spinning as it wobbled,
with 7 more leaning over
the rails of a smaller one
attached underneath,
spinning opposite -
word of mouth epochs
stacked below in mist
had the 7 screaming - their
Voice left to Vision and
the odd chance that I
might be the first in a
long while to take their bet

Doppler

Cowboy Cunt
Mother Nature
You Are Also
A Prick
For Fucking people
    And Also Suck
    For Chosing Who
    You Grab -
Your Fractal
Always Just
Far Enough Away
From De-Coding -
As If Helping Us
Would Be A Sin

I Bet There Was A Time
When You Did Not Exist

    When There Was No Sin

    Skin Was Not A Line

    Heart Not A Warrior

    And Breath Not Alone

And In That Time

The Savage Crystal Eye

Saw That All Were Protected

New York, New York

Blood Black Stallion
Heart Like A Wheel

You Act Like A Lamb

And A Snake

And A Man
Confused By His Hand
And What It Has
Done For Him Lately

because I am an asshole

----

because I am an asshole
I study selected asses
like there'll be a
written test to follow,
will not tell you
what I feel,
plow remorse,
ask for nothing
except relief
and call people "nuts"
convincingly...

because I am an asshole
I bad mouth you
behind your back for
bad mouthing me
behind mine,
ache with anxiety,
perk up my ears
only when you are
listening to me
and oppose anything
that gets on my nerves...

because I am an asshole
I condemn caprice,
judge glee,
shun the obvious
and watch you fall
rather than catch you,
then back-flip myself up
onto your shoulders when you
get up and attempt
to ride you like a camel...

because I am an asshole
I will squeeze continuity
from your gut,
let you slide without

explanation,
grunt when challenged
and forgive myself before
it has occurred to anyone else to…

because I am an asshole
I shiver when touched,
dispense caution reflexively,
warm right up to suggestion
and am a comfortable house guest
of Innocence when absolutely
necessary…

because I am an asshole
I leave the girls alone,
let the boys play,
duck advise,
run late for Wonder
and have forgotten more
than I remember about
propriety…

because I am an asshole
I mock heaven for arriving
without figuring out
a Drive-Thru,
rake Time with Science
when I am not feeling
holy,
push the river,
steal the sky,
save the souls
and say the word…

because I am an asshole
I purposely don't get out much –
in that way, limiting my exposure
to the rest of you assholes.

Vintage Gangsters

1990,
the year
every wine
from everywhere
was Brilliant!

line 'em up:
Lafite
Mouton
Haut Brion
Latour
Petrus
Leoville
Calon Segur
Palmer
Special Selection
Opus
Diamond Creek
Togni
Montebello
Montelena
Dominus…
"Line'em up!
We'll finish them
this sitting right
at Table 1.
Keep the Sous Chef
here 'til he cooks
the entire menu
for us and have the
Pastry Chef drop
a dozen deserts
at the bar, near
the Cognacs and
cigars!"

their names are mud,
the 'Fiduciary'
farts and burps
at this table
with a full mouth;
Executive Managers
laugh and burp
in tandem –
like they have
an audience
who bought tickets
to witness this, or
a jury to mock...

the doors have
long been locked
of course,
just to make sure
that they will
remain Alone –
the only way
these gems can
be savoured
without paying
for them.

Surprisingly,
I preferred the
Special Selection

liquorish

----

when I was a kid
   I liked the cherry
      the chocolate
         or even the strawberry
            but not the black
so now I like
   red Burgundy,
      juicy Bordeaux
        and consider myself
           quite luckied
              not to be sloshing Absinthe
                like a whore

Three-Eyed Johnny

Johnny 3 Eyes
bob weave cross
hook uppercut of Fate,
also duck suckerpunch
Identity

Watching while watching,
taken by no one,
as if he were God
and also wise,

he managed to stay clean
while sparring below the belt
and still get paid
like a winner after
every fix...

'til tagged by conscience
on the ropes of murder,
where he hung up gloves,
bloodied in victory...
just the way he pictured it
when he first stepped
into The Ring
and spotted the judges
down for the count
and the referee off
blowing someone
in the other corner

Our Gang

Retro Renfro Rifled
Refractions Like A
Rooster on a Hot
Recall Roof
Remedied Only
Running Into Rubber
Hitting Road
He Crowed Every Morning
Reasonably Doing What
Was To Be Done Dealing
Doped Disillate Of Distain
Along With Undeniable Will,
Who Wonked And Wastlanded
Awaited Wanderlust And Nick
Of Time Who Trip Drop-Kicked
Cradle, Knocking Heaven's Door –
Alone Wolff Bob Of Apple Annie,
Dunked 'Til Soaked Straight -
With Christian Crumb Begging
On Corner, Like John Without
Trick Of Eye To Flush Over Eddy,
Who Showed-Up Again
With Shill Bill, Later Please
And Skip, Who Remembers
Much More Has To Say

Flash Flooding Near San Jacinto

Lucky
To
Free
Love
Listen
Speak
Know
See
Eachother
Ourselves
The
Sky
Melt

Tibetan Jungle

"You Are Not
My Friend...
I Am Yours"

She Is My Guide Now
Stepping Back
To Her Place
Between Four Lamas
Who Open Cloths
Set In Front Of Them
Presenting Contents
In Reverent Posture

The Leaf, The Pen,
The Thunderbolt
And The Ornament –
       An Oval Suspended
       Inside A Circle
       Without Any Connection
       To The Circle
– The Charm Of Alchemy –

I Accept It
I Guess That I Can Even
Wear It If I Want To

I Understand That I Am
To Resist Infatuation
       ...and I do
           and I let it go
              and it is given to me

She Gives Me The Rest
Of The Stuff
With A Wave Of Her Hand
To The Lamas Who Lay Them
Before Me, Then Split, Backing
Out Bowing.

Young, Pretty Tibetan In
Western Pants And Crew
Sweater,
She Is At Ease With Appearance
And Liberation
Yet Consecrated To The Ancient
And The Duty She Has Been
Sent To Perform

Looking Back With Definite
Half-Smile, Almost Stern,
She Indictates Nothing
Except That I Have Been
Entrusted To Bring All
To The Temple Of Action –
That's Part Of The Deal -
      And That Just Because
      She Is Going To Be With Me,
      That Doesn't Mean That I
      Will Be With Her

I Think, "Not Yet, Anyway"

      Then She Splits In Slightest Skip
      One More Look Back

Uncle John's Band

Beauty spins
is spun
at the bottom of
this Age's barrel
      conning breath
      into Absolute wheels
      portioning mad epochs
      as quick as necessary

spilling mind/sense solution
sheens spirals of jester Time's
glitter mask that he demands
is flesh upon every penalty

pruned to discursive
at the stake,
awareness smokes with
Vision recognized in squints –
      fragments fed to consciousness
      as if they are something new -
      pulling the chain of civilizations
      one chimera at a time

      The Knower
      turns out and
      away to needy

      impoverished acceeding,
      The Fool pays for service
      and huddles around possession,
      as if his fist held water…

      at once, the Ring concedes
      itself and a hand,
      still through all dimension,
      is lifted

Salt March

----

by knowing
who I am
I come to a knife-fight
armed
with
a fucking
Bazooka

Courage!

who ever said that
there is something wrong
with poverty ?

Jesus was pretty poor
he only took down
the Roman Empire

Ghandi impoverished himself,
then he got The Brits

Abe Lincoln chopped wood

I'd bet Galileo's
grandparents
were Serfs

Mandela did not get new shoes every year

they say Buddha went without

Henry Miller worked
on Jay Street in Brooklyn

Allen Ginsburg sang for tea

Sufis are hi on rags

The Prophets only meal was Word

Patti Smith did not grow up
profiterolled

Mary Magdalene was not taken
from her boudoir

nothing ever came from something
something always comes of nothing

the open stare
of hope and wonder

is not dressed

mothers cannot escape birth

rivers take all to sea

Riches
know not this soul

"Don't Leave Me Yet.
I Have A Lot To Tell You"
(India)

Your Beloved's Breath
Becomes Your Heart –
Even If It Snores

Viva Roma!

You have to be Chinese
to understand Italians
'cause they just
don't give a shit

the rest of you
must suffer
under envy
and fall down
everytime you open your mouth
because you don't
know what you are
talking about...

Italians speak
fast to that issue
and will not
allow you
a moment
to recover
from your
own personal
bullshit

suggesting rapidly
a distractive venue
under strung lights
to dance This Night away...
or a charmed
ristorante
stream eternity
or Idea
from Dream
no mind

...or something else fast
...like a car
or a woman
or a man
or an Empire.

Queen's Jubilee

I am too old to eat

I had your lunch
thank you very much
just because
you are a goose
in a cage –
fattened without Taste –

I suppose
I will also take away
your dinner before
done
and quickly donate
the remains
to The Hungry
in My good name

you must work
for your breakfast
and fall cripple
on the way to table

if the eggs
are still warm,
perhaps that
will revive
my appetite

Breakfast at Norquist's

----

severed hand shake

        skeleton bun

Caesars due at any moment

              …and then some

    count me out in

Shit Donut

----

stuffed & fatted
choux fits
bag of
exhumed extrusions
rove
fox-stilled
surface waters
like frankenscum at play
on scalia motor-mouth skis
that also suck....

dunkin' heiny faces
squirt their jam
when squeezed
just like the
Big Bakers prepped them;
swarming kellogged corpulents
to ooze scent.

power switched remote,
paddle spun dough
hardens like glue
from dream horses
once galloped.

Deep In The Topanga Canyon

oliveloaf twofer
forgetmenot Not
sweat pasture retirement
hung low
and dangled
for vipers
even at that rate

no house Home
underwater
Grow Fins Quick
sell your silver

your long-banked
student bodies jammed
from behind -
tricks
for rent
crammed by the hour

BigBuy SellOut
bounty hunts
Great Society
for kicks
penalties heap
at all shelter gates
as if The Invisible
could also disappear

Feeling itself is gentrified,
as still-bristled Straights,
probably the only 65 yr.olds
able to actually remember
The Hippie Revolution,
(that, for being spectators)
dispense their easy to be hard,
Still Jealous avarice
from benches, pulpits
lecterns and power...
all the while mouthing
they won't get fooled again.

Distant Thunder

----

we eat pills
because there
is no rice

somewhere along
the Supply-Side
we contracted-out freedom
to hi low-life bidders
scrambling for take
boot camp to black bag
making hay
while the sun
don't shine…
and nobody hears
but the Forgotten -
marching single file
like ants in dirt hole,
boiling river water
poured on them
every odd second
and they keep
marching back
as soon as it dries
even just a little bit.

'Generation Hessian'
also has blood
family
friend…
once had no job
like you
no health insurance
like you
no hope
like you…
no more -
dead-end sifted -
'safety net' raised like Golem tent -
they are Enlisted
then exploded by Whim
while out for a 4th of July morning walk

a little help from our friends

**"*Free* Photo I.D. For Voting
Available At Your Local D.M.V."**

                  drag your chains with you
                  to the back of a bus…or 2…or 3
                  …but no Saturday or Sunday –
                  only on a workday, just in case you
                  need the money.
                        please get there at least
                        two hours early so you
                        can watch us watching
                        you.
      don't forget all
      documents…especially
      birth certificate.
            if you never got one
           or it was washed away
         in the flood, or burned in
        the fires – you'll have to
       contact the hospital
       by certified mail
       or town clerk archive
-this may take a while –
    at least 'til after
    nov.6…
      but if you do have one,
      we will need written proof
      along with your mother's
      birth certificate, an affidavit
      signed by a court-appointed
      trustee
         stating that your father
         is or was a male…
         attached also must be
         his last 6 month's pay stubs,
         fingerprints and or dna sample
      don't forget to bring
      your last 18 month's
      cancelled checks and
      cable bills,

disposition of all felonies,
all preferred shopper's cards
(all sku's must scan!)
  if you are disabled,
  weak or meek or ill
                    you must hire a taxi
                    (you will be responsible
                    for all freight)
if you happen
to use the internet,
we require a non-returnable
zip-drive loaded with your complete
e-mail files witnessed, inspected
and delivered 5 days in advance
by sheriff.

                    upon arrival
                    at dmv
                    take a number
                    for a number...
                    wait for them to
                    be called, lit
                    or stamped
                    when all windows
                    are back from lunch
don't eat
hope for
the best
        and if you
        miss your ride
        home
            walk.

supply side
----

middle class heritage
and dream
ate by John Birch ilks
laughing with malice
all the way to their banks

as we watch
the world pass by
again
as if we are kids again

but now there ain't
no mama no papa
no uncle
or anything like that…
no doctor who knew
your grandmother,
no people out on
the street looking-out
for the neighborhood,
no cop but fear,
no court that has not
been taken,
no name for war,
no Voice for Peace,
no pride,
no grace,
no Tenderness…

simply Us – on our own
with the quiet, craven
warden of "Austerity"
and the echo
of bigger threats
that also
'could never happen
here'

Gavone

----

always unkempt
can't stop eating…
make a mess
leave clean-up
for daft
and slave

talk cheap
but spree
anytime
for right price
daring Time itself
to forsake you
at it's own peril

of judgement hand
vengeance sword
'grail' tounged
enforcer
army of
ephemora
tablet armoured
god of each direction

step stood still

you come like a fever
complete with the chill

your name is
Morality –
the empty heart
shill.

Wretched Camp

----

school is out
childsplay
turns on forest,
meadow, river
and lake –
"Good To Go"
for a little Take –
and not much Give,
but lipservice

uniformed ones
corral the capped,
kerchiefed and
medalled troops –
marched for outing,
hiked 'til skirmished
against lines of law –
where they make a fire
before native and nature
has had a chance to breathe,
then sing loud around the flames
songs of Oath, Congratulations
and Prayer
roasting what meat
and marshmellows
thcy have left...
until lullabye of stars
rocks them
stuck sleeping in Bags
dreaming of a
Big Breakfast

Wall Mart

strip frack machu picchu melon balls
ming hung macaroon
pitch black label
prime beef
christian mingled yeast snacks
blister sleeve private parts
russian dressing
korean darts
wheeled chairs hover
gadgets gum pumps
flat screen floss flowers
plaid shirt pants and
all beverage flapped left of
contacts, pedicures, pretzels
and pills:

everything available
by treaty
by war
by law
by sneak
by pressure
on demand

3 cents, 4 cents,
occasionally a dime cheaper
and the rare dollar loss-leader,
all gathered in one tent
precision pitched before
you hit your town.

quizno'd goblets,
ranchero-thighed,
roam parking lot in
hip-hobble, cellulosed,
high jinx trek
to mobile cart clutching

of clockworked
cramps, scars, hives
and rashes stacked like deck –
shrink wrap shining –
picked, packed and sent
by distant forgotten
haunting each easy grip

blue vested weight lung
Associates
droop the floor
cranked with survival
as doors sting open
non-stop…

      at these prices,
      who can resist?

Quiet Years On The Strip

Nothing is missing

Circle lost Spot

Beat cannot inhale

The Dialogue bounces

Dance does not weep,

nor Theater cry.

Paint dare not

Earth goes flat

Work steep,

boots hedged

sleep walked

no home alone

Postman ringing...
                    make that twice.

Chance Luberon

----

summer strong
cool breeze chops
flamenco sharp chase
of sun and shade
dimension and palette
at once frame
and mirror
spinning
in high fury
strobe swirled
tall tree waves.

blow this page away
and I could be anywhere
... mostly Provence
where everything simple fits
and hill piles pleasure
in clear valley sight...
but I know where I am -
unpacking car Residence Inn
Bergen County,
en route to my
week at 'Jersey Shore'.
no complaints...
only that I am fool
again to think that
memory can conjure
verisimilitude -
there won't be
any Cavaillon...
lucky for cantaloupe.
flounder my dourade -
salsa my tapenade
jerky my jambon
chili daube
'sauce' ratatouille
button cepe
Dunkin' galette
'submarine' pan bagna
taco socca
pepperoni saucisson

philly cheese carpaccio
'regular' cafe
'sundae' profiterole
zambucca pastis
vodka pineau
vodka rose'
deli marche'
drive thru dejeuner
byob
nightclub night
in no Cap
beach flatline stretch
nude strapped cop-tight
hot dogged
where light
is heat
lavender aerosol
rose not a rose
lawn mow
for wild thyme
tout le jour
     belch when asked
     speak no language
     and don't forget
     your beach pass...
so I guess I'll
scramble the ol' oeuf
encore and boardwalk-back
vacation 'til it hurts...
     yet, out behind
     crisscrossed branches
     of parking lot perimeter,
Gehry-like
blackout eves
of sunken office building
assume the position
in uncanny Plateau Vaucluse mimick.

I bench sit ponder
long minutes
fuzzed back
to vineyard outside Aix

swarmed by that
same prehistoric Mont outline
as if it were today,
then room retire
somewhat encouraged
that something Poetic
might happen
this vacation-time around.

At night I dream about a flesheater who is eating my flesh - you know - restraining me; pulling my eyeball out; hacking at my chest; buzz-sawing my shins, etc., etc., etc. in a dim lit room I keep escaping from into the downtown of a Madrid-like city, only to be caught every time and appear back in the room for more slaughter - the mad glossy-eyed Cheshire-cat-faced sadist cannibal tongue flaring, slicing my flesh more - wide clown smile cackling behind my screams...

he ate like a coon and smelled like chopped beef; said he stayed on the Isle St. Louis coming up.

He stripped down to his way too small jockey
underwear frequently while jostling water hoses, syringes and clamps - bragged with hideous laugh that he was a Fat Bastard before he was a Fat Bastard - then he bit off a chunk of my cheek like an apple.

He tickled himself railing that he hated people who work for a living, so he hired some.

He waddled like a pig if pig's could waddle; made lavender his fat sock color bulging along with his fat feet from $4000 loafers

He chicken-scissored the ligaments & tendons between 4 of my toes...
then he stepped back to admire his work...
little fat guy with slicked back hair and a silly suit
...his cohorts said he came out of the West -
Texas or thereabouts...
they called him Chance ...
Chance Luberon.

Pigeon Hole

They steal your life
just to flex their favor

They take it
and they keep it

and if they catch
you smiling
They quick remind
you that They will
never give it back…
no matter who
you are Becoming.

The Child,
never stillborn
sings the soul
of the Friend
from each
heartbeat's alley,

diverting forgotten eyes
hid looking for an echo
in the big, blue, silent sky.

Overview

Life Blows
　　　With Grace
Sucks
　　　With A Feeling
Goes On
　　　With Abandon
Is Good
　　　When Not Better

　　　　　...used to be a cereal
　　　　　...and a magazine

　　　　　　　still a sentence
　　　　　　　an expectancy
　　　　　　　a bitch...

is bigger
insured
threatened
affirmed
saved
　　　and droned
lay low

The Pitch Of Alchemy

Nothing *will do*
yet
Triumph
snaps
sleep of Appearance
bargain of Belief
gloom of Expectation
question of Time
and
riddle of Exile

The Curve Of Pursuit

----

races run
like signals surf
in Conjure striptease…
the fast stream slow stop,
squarely unbreaking The Circle on the way.

sandbox beached
Healing hand touched
Divined unearthed dug-in

shoe walked a mile in fits
on Victory's lap…
hush rhapsody whispering
sung song singing

"How Do You Get
To Carnegie Hall?"
…Listen

Kingdom Come

If you can forgive yourself

you can forgive them

Karma

The Robot is not judgemental
don't bother asking It for favors
You did not build It to listen
but only to Act

It passes You by
in the split between
the second You turn It on
and the seed of Your memory -

particulate of desire
ghost of thought
rubicon of illusion
atom-hard skin of hunger
reason's blunt simitar
assassin paid in Time –

You, hypnotist hypnotized
even gave It a nickname: Karma –

as if It were
your pet

…how fitting

You Make My Dreams Come True

who'd a thunk
it would be you ?
6 foot, no ass,
horseface, bucktooth,
bad attitude,
blowhard
in 'Loner' drag
a little too slick…

scared and scary,
smiling only when
finally and
excruciatingly amused…
or gifted…

gawky gait
unzipped
daft foot soldier
of Nothingness,
parading like
a bitch of a
Beast Of Burden
down this avenue
no stone unturning –
baking cake eating it –
"rocking the boat" to sleep –
ringing Silence bell
overending
loudly
        in a room right
        next to mine…

                bare and untouched,
                you have my full
                attentions now,
        oh long suffering Genie
        in the looking glass…

        your 3 wishes please

****

I saw a Fool
I handed him down
miles for cover
shit for brains
polished brass for balls
panned gold for heart

caveat emptor 2015

I bothered to listen in
on as many conversations
as I could yesterday

I heard nothing

didn't people used to say,
"What's Happening"
like they knew?

or "Oh Wow!"
with marvel celebration?

or even "Groovy"
to a groove?
…forget about
" What It Is "
(street existential)
or "What Is It"
(street existential backwards)

these days, they pigeon "coo"
for Cool… "very cool"
for gudgingly acceptable
and that ain't cool

or feign commiseration
with the downward
glance:
"Interesting"
for:
I don't give
a rat's ass
what you say

or "no worries"-
like you better
start worrying
right away
or *"Actually"*
like Fuck You

but like I said,
I didn't hear nothin'
did you???

Actually
that's coo
very cool
no worries

Interesting

Preachers Always
Have Dog Breath
----

if every road
was the road not taken
we might get somewhere

a wish never fulfilled
might have done you a favor

what you think is required
might disqualify you

      sunset has no problem
      sunrise has no pride

            a question
            unanswered
            has answered

            a word misplaced
            is a clue

            revelation
            is gumption's
            breath

            mandatory
            only exists
            in the absence
            of necessity

      passion does
      not plead

      rivers rush
      anonymous

strangers given
sustainance
grow blood
thicker than water

a demand ignored
is a door opened

the crest
of silence
glimmers

by now
you may be
getting my drift,

so please take
your seats…

Sublime

----

it's a mystery to me how
anyone knows anything
about The Hereafter…

nevermind The Here

Perhaps

Perhaps if Greed
were not
Fear itself
it would have
a different name
...like 'Plenty'
and not need
War for sustainence
nor weapons of Time
and Politic
to secure and sanction
bury and exhume.

Perhaps if Compassion
were not
enshrined
it would have
a different name
...like, 'Survival'
and we would
eat, walk and sleep
like humankind
imagined -
in Peace.

Perhaps if Individuality
were not a code
and oath
it would have
a different name...
like, 'Particle'
that our
command performanced egos
would adopt
with relief
and begin
to finally
embrace
Harmony.

Perhaps
if Knowledge
were not
a zero sum race
flourished,
it would have
a different name…
like, 'Song'
and stop
lepering
Wisdom,
thus hearing
the Kind Dervish's
breath
and heartbeat
precognate
a New Age.

Perhaps,
even in Alchemy,
'one thing leads to another'
and we can make a move…

Everybody Been Somewhere

----

look close
everyone
gives it away
every movement
every glance -
even the sly
are antsy -
side-eye sensing
that what they
are doing
they already done
somehow someway
and with each breath
do some more -
everybody's trippin'
watchin' themselves
watch themselves -
a performance -
script shot in blood
before memory -
yet we feel -
just at arm's length -
something almost familiar -
behind us
in front
all around -
beckoning -
a double
a twin
a friend
a secret with thrill attached.

each time
we verge
on it's exquisite hint,
we are Voyager
ready the same -
only to be
impassed

by the mystery
of Thought...
sorta like
tryin' to lift
an old girlfriend's skirt
when she is wearing,
and swears she has
always worn
pants.

Baksheesh

----

a perfect summer day
is a bribe
attempting to
garner favor
for Kindness

waving to a particle

----

you aren't there
      'til you are here
           neither is anything else

what's behind me
      I project
         from when
            it was in front
what's in front
      I conjured
         at the same instant
         I covered my tracks;
               leaving The Circle Broken,
               The Way exposed
               in shadowplayed
               silent spiral
               glistened revolutions
               without a cause…

…yet streaming high up and right over this hidden deep well of Science, an outsized, very long-necked, splendiferous iridescent bird, plowing the landscape psychedelic with each waft of enormous wingspan, squawks big beak and craps simultaneous.

The Elixir Of Breeze

8 Beauties Spin Clockwise
Over 12 Prophets
Revolving Counter
Atop 3 Kings
Perched On Balconies,
Wise Men At Side,
Overlooking Courtyards
Of Pilgrims, Devotees
And Mendicants –
Priests At The Corners,
Dressing Walls Of
Images And Words
Incomprehensible –
And A Door Or 2
At The Back
From Which
Every Single One
Of Them,
Each In Their
Own Turn,
Swivel
Bow
Then
Split.

"Yes, we have lemons"

You drove me to eye surgery today
singing 'Wake Up Little Suzie'

You picked me up later
with my cool Surgery Center issue shades
after the best Psychedlic experience
since 'California Sunshine'
singing 'Walk Right Back'

You dropped me home to chill,
shopped, crapped the dog twice, got
my brand new Medicare card laminated,
came back with bundles from the farmer's
market, loaded 50 years of my poetry
onto a zip-drive, let me massage your back,
noticed my black Lauren shoes after 4 years,
finished your real estate messages, cooked
your Miracle Lamb Ragu, then baked
an organic apple galette from scratch,
went for a ride with the dog and called
me 1/2 hour later, sounding slightly
alarmed, to see if we had lemons
for your Caesar dressing…

the day after your bone marrow biopsy
came back OK after a month of weeks
of exhaustion, antibiotics, radioactive pills
and thyroid scans, brainscans, bone density
testing, MRAs, breast biopsy, 1/2 dozen blood tests
and finally the liver test to decide how carefully
to go forward with your treatment…

Yes, my dear one
of all these years – we do
have lemons…
and perhaps even
lemonade

The Healer

When Love Is All That Is Left
Take Your Hat Off And Stay For Awhile
Where You've Always Been –
Old, Wise And Able To Heal
With Hand, Mind And Vision –
You Were Not Taught This
But Given It Whole In A Moment
When Love Was All That Was Left

Dal Lake

I am tall tree in it's branches
reflected on still lake
by moon shining full behind me

night clouds sail by above,
gestating the image –
light shuttered defracted,
then exposed
waving with my limbs
above the water
that has captured
all of us
in vivid locket
alluring contemplation
as The Pilgrim
approaches it's banks

The Old Croak

----

the old croak
went to bed
with The Princess
and woke up older
but he had forgotten

then they had kids
who do not need memory
and a dog
who knew all
their names

one day they went
to the store
and found bugs
in their cheese
if anyone was alarmed
no one knew
but the manager
who offered his first
daughter up
and they all accepted
without predjudice
because his daughter
had 3 legs
and 2 noses.

back at the house
they played like mice
and ate like lions
until the corn was gone

parent/teacher night
was not a problem since
all in attendance
had degrees
in audio/visual -
secrets could not
be a problem...

in general,
nothing was...
until the rabbit
shot the tortoise
with valium
and things started
to really slow-down

things got so slow
that time passed by

the old croak
went to bed
with The Princess
and woke up older
but he had forgotten

The Wail Next Door

Fear of Fear
Terror of Vengeance
Hatred of Rule
Secret of Pain
Shame of Confusion
Guilt of Escape

Stricken with Humility
Shy a Few Bones
Racked Like a Cow
Born Without a Hug
Grown on Fire

Passed to Strangers
Caught in Passion
Strangled by Desire
Stammering at Touch
Singled Out with No
Witness Witnessing

Crammed into a Hole
the Size of a Pin
as Big as The World
and as Deep
as the Sea
that He
Must Drown
Everyday

Until We Meet Again

Palanquin Of Dust
Embossed With Every Breath -
Roads Run Walked,
Carried In Your Bed
By Servants Of Grace
Given To Faith
By Courage
In Love -

Remain

.

www.ingramcontent.com/pod-product-compliance
Lightning Source LLC
Chambersburg PA
CBHW031143090426
42738CB00008B/1192